Cornerstones of Freedom

The Story of
THE FLIGHT AT
KITTY HAWK

By R. Conrad Stein

Illustrated by Len W. Meents

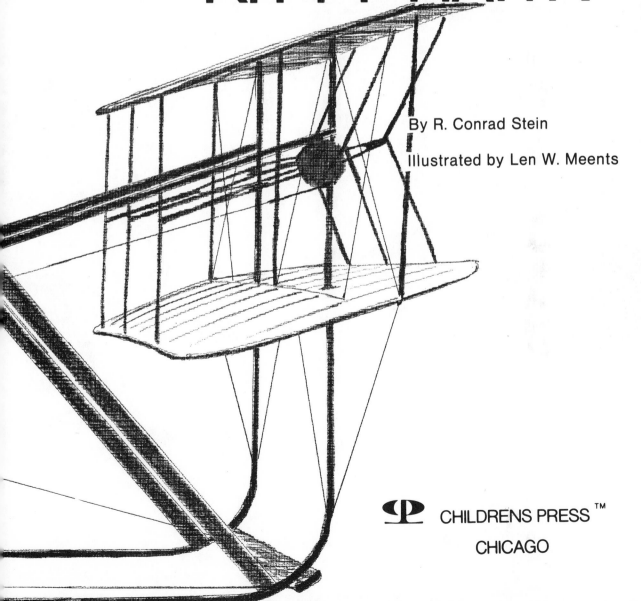

CHILDRENS PRESS™

CHICAGO

Library of Congress Cataloging in Publication Data

Stein, R. Conrad.
  The story of the flight at Kitty Hawk.

  (Cornerstones of freedom)
  Summary: A brief biography of the two famous
bicycle makers from Dayton, Ohio, focusing on their
efforts to build and fly an airplane, starting with
kites and gliders.
  1. Wright, Orville, 1871-1948—Juvenile literature.
2. Wright, Wilbur, 1867-1912—Juvenile literature.
[1. Wright, Orville, 1871-1948. 2. Wright, Wilbur,
1867-1912. 3. Aeronautics—Biography] I. Meents,
Len W. II. Title. III. Series.
TL540.W7S7   629.13'00922 [B] [920]   81-1634
  ISBN 0-516-04614-4   AACR2

On a cold December morning two brothers walked up a hill in North Carolina. On top of that hill sat a strange-looking contraption. It was held together with wooden poles and baling wire. Muslin cloth covered most of the frame. The brothers were Orville and Wilbur Wright. On that morning they hoped to do something that had never been done before. They were going to try to fly an airplane.

The Wright brothers were bicycle makers from Dayton, Ohio. They had built an aircraft called the *Flyer*. It was made up almost entirely of two large wings. Mounted on the bottom wing was a gasoline engine. That engine could deliver about as much power as one of today's heavy-duty lawnmowers. The engine drove two bicycle chains. The chains, in turn, drove the craft's two propellers.

Orville and Wilbur flipped a coin to see who would be the first to try to fly. Wilbur won the flip. He climbed onto the *Flyer*. To work the controls, he lay on his stomach between the double wings.

Now all was ready.

The engine rattled. The propellers whirled. Two small boys and a dog who had come to watch were suddenly frightened. They scampered away. The *Flyer* sat on a wooden railing that served as a takeoff ramp. The ramp slanted downhill. A restraining wire held the aircraft in place. With its propellers spinning madly, the *Flyer* tugged at the wire like a dog on a leash. Wilbur nodded to his brother, and Orville released the wire.

The *Flyer* lunged forward and rolled down the ramp. For thirty-five feet, Orville ran alongside, holding the wing tip for balance. Then he let go. He stopped and held his breath. The aircraft carrying his brother actually lifted from the ramp! But, quick as an eye blink, it thumped down into the dirt. The Wright brothers' first attempt at powered, heavier-than-air flight had failed. The date of that first attempt was December 14, 1903.

The Wrights were not discouraged. They discussed what repairs were needed on the *Flyer*. Then they pushed their aircraft back up the hill. They would try again in a few days. History would have to wait.

Manned flight was not new at the time. Balloons had been carrying men into the skies for more than

one hundred years. Balloons, however, flew only
because the gases inside them made them lighter
than air. Once aloft, they drifted with the winds.
They were practically impossible to control.

Gliders were another method of flying at the time. They were lightweight craft with long wingspans. Hundreds of gliders were being built and flown in Europe and America. To fly a glider, the pilot and one or two assistants usually ran down a hill holding the glider over their heads. When the wings began to lift the glider up, the pilot would jump aboard. He would be happy to fly a few feet. Once in the air, glider pilots had very little control over their craft.

The Wright brothers had been outstanding builders and flyers of gliders. But now they were attempting something quite different. They hoped to fly a powered, heavier-than-air machine in a flight controlled by the pilot. This was something brand-new.

Most people thought they were mad. A flying machine can't work, the brothers were told. It's impossible.

But a handful of scientists and engineers believed that such a machine could be built. One of them was a respected American scientist named Samuel Pierpont Langley. Mr. Langley was an officer of the famous Smithsonian Institution in Washington, D.C.

In the laboratories of the Smithsonian, Langley had built many models of heavier-than-air flying machines. The models looked something like large dragonflies. One of these models was powered by a small steam engine. It had flown the incredible distance of three-quarters of a mile. Langley was overjoyed with the flight. Now all he had to do was build a larger model and put a man in it.

The United States Army was interested in Langley's aircraft. They gave him $50,000 to continue his work. Langley also received a $20,000 grant from the Smithsonian Institution. In those days, $70,000 was a fortune. Langley was able to buy modern equipment. He was able to hire technicians to help him build his flying machine. He could also send for the latest reports on flying experiments that were taking place around the world.

Meanwhile, the Wright brothers worked alone. They couldn't afford to hire help. To buy equipment, they had only the money saved from their small bicycle shop in Dayton. Instead of the latest reports, they had to study books and pamphlets on aviation. Some of these were borrowed from the Dayton Public Library. Others had been sent to them by the Smithsonian.

Langley's machine was ready in October of 1903, only a short time before the Wright brothers' *Flyer* was ready. Langley called his machine the *Aerodrome*. Its first test was a failure. But on December 8, 1903, Langley was ready to try again.

Like the Wrights' craft, the *Aerodrome* would be launched from a rail. But Langley mounted his rail on the roof of a houseboat in the Potomac River. The aircraft was supposed to land in the river. The pilot was a young engineer. He stripped down to his long underwear before boarding the *Aerodrome*. Since he would have to swim to shore, he did not want to be weighted down by heavy clothing.

At a signal from Langley, the *Aerodrome* was released. It shot down the rail over the houseboat. When it reached the end of the rail, it nosed over and plunged directly into the river. The pilot had to be fished out of the icy water.

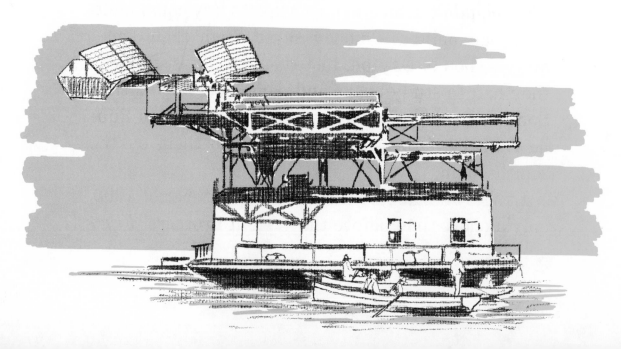

Newspapers blasted Langley's failure. They said he had wasted $70,000 of taxpayers' money building a machine that could never fly. One newspaper called the *Aerodrome* a "Mud Duck." Another newspaper said, "Perhaps if the professor had only thought to launch his airship bottom up, it would have gone into the air instead of down into the water."

In North Carolina, Orville and Wilbur Wright were saddened to read about Langley's failure. They felt a common bond with Langley. He was one of the few people in the world trying to achieve powered flight. He had the same dream of flying that Wilbur and Orville Wright had always had.

Perhaps the start of the Wright brothers' dream could be traced back to their childhood.

When Orville Wright was seven years old and his brother eleven, their father returned from a business trip. With him he brought an unusual toy.

"Look, boys," he said, and threw them the toy.

But this toy did not fall to the floor. Instead, it flew straight up and fluttered about the ceiling before it fell. It was a tiny helicopter made of cork, paper, and bamboo. The toy was powered by a twisted rubber band. It had been made in France.

The Wright brothers played with the helicopter for two days. Then it broke. They tried to build a larger model from cardboard boxes. But they could not get it to fly.

Years later, however, these two brothers would get many hundreds of their models to fly.

In school both boys were very bright. But neither of them liked to sit for long hours in the classroom. Wilbur was a superb athlete until he developed a heart disorder which kept him indoors. So he spent many hours reading and dabbling with mechanical projects. Orville was far more active. He loved to ride things. He especially enjoyed speeding over the streets on a bicycle.

Neither of the Wright boys went to college. Wilbur hoped to earn money as an inventor. Orville opened a tiny print shop. They were both going broke when they decided to open a bicycle shop.

In just a few years the bicycle shop was a success. Both brothers were gifted mechanics. They designed a sturdy bike that could be made for less money than others on the market. Soon they were making and selling enough bicycles to earn a comfortable living. Best of all, they had some free time during the winter months when not many people rode bikes.

The Wrights used their free time to study the fascinating problems and possibilities of flight.

First they studied the birds that glided over the Ohio countryside. Orville later wrote, "We could not understand that there was anything about a bird that would enable it to fly that could not be built on a larger scale and used by man." Watching the birds made the Wright envious. They, too, wanted to fly gracefully in the air. After hours of discussion, they decided to build a glider.

The Wrights began by flying kites. Since they hoped to graduate to gliders, they built their kites to look like small gliders. While delighted neighborhood children watched, they flew these kites in empty lots in Dayton.

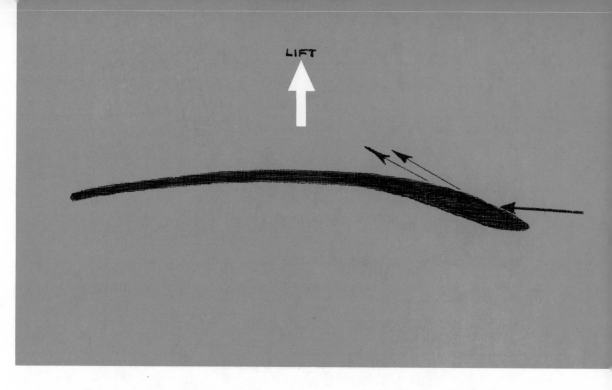

From the beginning, the two brothers tried to control their kites while they were in the air. They were sure that a glider could achieve longer flights if the pilot were in control.

While struggling with the problem of control, Wilbur hit upon a most important idea. The idea had to do with a warped wing. A warped wing is a wing that is curved on the top. The Wrights knew that when air flows over a warped wing it provides what is called "lift." Lift, they knew, would carry a glider off the ground. Why not, thought Wilbur, let the pilot of the glider control the warp of each wing? Then, if the glider started dipping to the left, the pilot could increase the warp of the left wing. That would increase the lift of that wing and straighten out the craft. Ropes could be attached to each wing. The glider pilot could pull on those ropes to change the warp of the wings.

Wilbur rushed to find his brother and explain to him this new idea.

They immediately began working long hours building a kite to test the new idea. This kite had a five-foot wing span. Lines hung down from the tip of each wing. These lines gave the man on the ground control over the wing warp. The kite worked! By continuing to change the warp of each wing, the Wrights had complete control over the kite as it sailed in the wind. If they wished, they could make the kite do a dance in midair.

The Wrights had achieved wing warping. Up to that time, it was the most important single breakthrough in the progress of flight. Now they began to build a glider using the principle of wing warping. Such a glider should be able to fly farther than any other glider had flown before.

They would have to find the best place in the country to fly the finished glider. Gliders need wind to get off the ground. So an ideal location would be one where the wind blows almost constantly. The Wrights wrote to the United States Weather Bureau asking for suggestions. The Bureau recommended a spot near a beach in North Carolina. There a steady breeze blew in off the Atlantic Ocean. The area was near a tiny town with the odd name of Kitty Hawk. Wilbur went to Kitty Hawk. He discovered a hundred-foot sand dune there with the even odder name of Kill Devil Hill. The dune rose over a field of rocks, weeds, and blowing sand. It was a strange place for history to be made.

In the fall of 1900, the Wright brothers boarded a train for North Carolina. With them was a huge box. It contained the disassembled glider they had built in their bicycle shop.

Living in a tent near Kill Devil Hill, the Wright brothers began gliding. They took turns piloting their glider, and they discovered the thrill of flight. Lying face downward, they were able to watch the ground rush past below them as their glider soared through the air. The feeling of flight was like a waking dream.

Built into the Wrights' first glider was the wing warping system they had tested on their kites. It worked even better than they had expected. But their glides were still very short. They lasted only five to ten seconds and covered distances of only twenty or thirty feet.

Next year, the brothers decided, they would build a better glider.

At home in Dayton, the Wrights built a wind tunnel. It was a box open at both ends. At one end the Wrights placed a fan driven by a gasoline engine. The fan created a steady "wind" inside the box. The brothers then placed model gliders in the box. The models were wired to the sides of the box so they appeared to float in the center. Watching different-shaped models inside the wind tunnel helped the Wrights design their second glider.

Orville and Wilbur returned to Kitty Hawk in 1901. With them they had a new glider. This one was a great success. In it they broke the world record for glider flight by soaring 389 feet.

In 1902 they brought an even more improved glider to Kitty Hawk. This craft had a new rudder control. Orville Wright was becoming an excellent pilot. He discovered that he could achieve a very stable flight by combining wing warping with proper movement of the rudder. This greater stability enabled their glider to soar the undreamed-of distance of more than 600 feet.

Because of their success in gliding, a very important man visited the Wrights. He was a famous and wealthy engineer named Octave Chanute. When he was in his sixties, Chanute retired from business to devote his energy to flight. He had built and flown many gliders. He had also written one of the books on flying machines that the Wrights had studied.

Mr. Chanute was amazed when he saw one of the Wright gliders perform at Kitty Hawk. He wondered how the brothers had built such a remarkable craft. They were half his age, they lacked his engineering experience, and they had never been to college. Yet these two young men had built the best glider in the world.

"You can go no further in gliding," Chanute told the Wrights. "Now all you can do is put a motor on that glider of yours and fly it."

Wilbur and Orville nodded. For many months they had been discussing doing exactly that.

But first they needed a suitable motor.

The Wrights wrote to several auto companies. They discovered that none of them built an engine light enough to mount on an airframe. So they had to construct their own engine in the Dayton shop. They studied library books and experimented with different designs. Then they built a four-cylinder gasoline engine that weighed about 150 pounds.

Next they needed a propeller.

Other designers of flying machines had thought of the propeller as sort of an airscrew. The airscrew would push an aircraft through the air the same way a ship's propeller pushes the ship through the water. The Wright brothers thought of their propeller as a moving wing. They believed it should be designed with a curved top and a flat bottom. With that design, the air rushing over the spinning propeller would supply lift the way a wing does. Therefore, the propeller should drive the aircraft forward the same way a wing lifts it off the ground.

Again the Wrights' theories were correct. Propellers today are built according to the same principles the Wrights understood eighty years ago.

The two brothers spent hours and hours discussing the details of their aircraft. They often had heated disagreements. Many nights they sat up late in the kitchen of their father's house in Dayton. They pored over drawings and argued till dawn. No one brother really won these arguments. As Orville once wrote, "Often, after an hour or so of heated argument, we would discover that we were as far from agreement as when we started, *but that each of us had changed to the other's position.*"

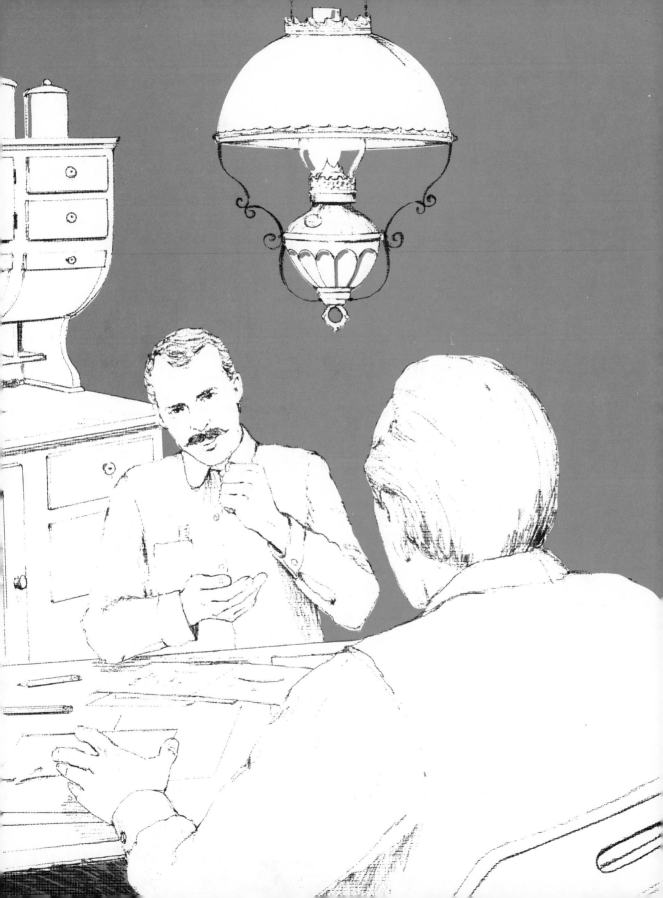

On the morning of December 17, 1903, everything was ready for the second trial of the Wright brothers' flying machine.

It was cold. Puddles of standing water had frozen during the night. A brisk 27-mile-an-hour wind was blowing. Wilbur and Orville walked up Kill Devil Hill where the *Flyer* waited to be launched. Perhaps the brothers could smell success in the wind that morning. They summoned five men from the nearby Life Saving Station. These men would help them launch the *Flyer*. They would also be witnesses to the flight. The Wrights even gave one of the men a camera. They asked him to snap a picture the moment the *Flyer* lifted into the air.

At ten-thirty that morning Wilbur started the engine. It was now Orville's turn to pilot the *Flyer*. Wilbur had had his chance during the unsuccessful attempt three days earlier. As the engine rattled, the brothers shook hands. Some sort of electricity must have passed between Orville and Wilbur Wright. Years later, one of the five witnesses reported, "We couldn't help notice how they held onto each other's hand, sort of like they hated to go; like two folks parting who weren't sure they'd ever see each other again."

Finally Orville climbed on board the *Flyer*. He lay face down on the bottom wing. He signaled to his brother that he was ready.

Wilbur took his place. He held the wing off the ground because the *Flyer* tended to lean that way on the launching rail. One of the men released the restraining wire. The *Flyer* rolled forward—faster, faster, faster. Then, in one breathtaking instant, it rose off the launching rail and Orville Wright flew into history.

On this frozen field a man and a machine had rivaled the birds.

That moment will never be forgotten. But that first flight carried Orville only 120 feet—about half the length of a football field. Their gliders had done better.

Years later Orville wrote, "The flight lasted only twelve seconds, but it was nevertheless the first time in the history of the world in which a machine carrying a man had raised itself by its own power into the air in full flight . . ."

The brothers flew their aircraft three more times that day. Wilbur piloted the *Flyer* on the last flight. It carried him a spectacular 852 feet and lasted fifty-nine seconds.

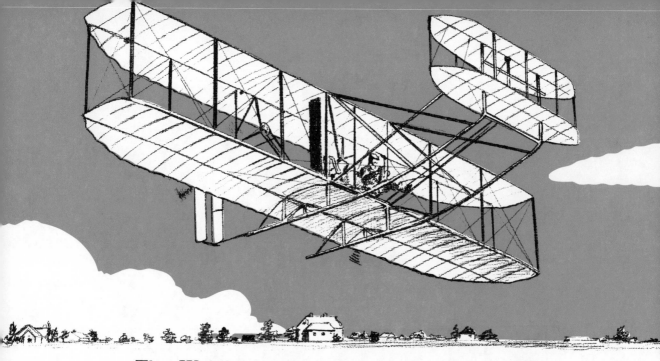

The Wright brothers had made history. But it would be a long time before the world learned what had taken place at Kitty Hawk. Strangely, American newspapers did not seem interested in man's first flight. The Wrights reported the story, but most papers did not bother to carry it. The papers that did print the story reported it inaccurately. One newspaper even published an absurd drawing of what they claimed the flying machine looked like. The drawing showed a sort of car perched on a huge propeller. The paper claimed that the propeller gave the car elevation.

The Wright brothers packed up the *Flyer* and went home to Dayton. There they built and tested more airplanes. By 1905 they had perfected an amazing craft. It would fly twenty-five miles in dis-

tance, stay aloft for half an hour, and reach a speed of forty miles an hour. And the pilot had perfect control over this aircraft. If he wished, he could fly in circles, or even figure eights.

Gradually the world discovered the miracle that these two brothers had created. In 1908, Wilbur and his aircraft sailed to France. There the Ohio bicycle maker stunned the French public with one dazzling flying exhibition after another. Soon all of Europe wanted to see the flying machine built by the two Americans. At home, the United States Army became interested in buying aircraft made by the Wrights.

In 1909 the brothers formed the Wright Company. They opened a factory in Dayton to produce aircraft. Orders for their marvelous machines came from all over the world. The Wright brothers had spent years working only for the love of flying. Now they finally began to earn money for their efforts.

Wilbur Wright, whose health had always been poor, died of typhoid fever in 1912. He did not live long enough to see the undreamed-of advances made in the field of aviation. Orville Wright lived until 1948. He saw airplanes speed into the dawn of the jet age.

Orville also saw aircraft used in war. This was a development he had not expected. It saddened him deeply. In 1917, while World War I raged in Europe, Orville wrote, "When my brother and I built and flew the first man-carrying flying machine, we thought we were introducing into the world an invention which would make further wars practically impossible."

Twenty-nine years after the flight at Kitty

Hawk, a huge granite memorial was dedicated to the genius of the Wright brothers. It stands on Kill Devil Hill, where history was made one cold morning in December.

There is another memorial to the Wright brothers in the National Air and Space Museum in Washington, D.C. That museum is part of the Smithsonian Institution. The original Wright *Flyer* hangs from the ceiling of the Air and Space Museum. It is the same machine that carried Orville Wright on his historic 1903 flight.

After that flight, the *Flyer* became a well-traveled museum piece. For some years it was displayed at the Massachusetts Institute of Technology near Boston. In 1928 it went to England for display at the London Science Museum. The aircraft remained there for the next twenty years. During World War II, the British stored the *Flyer* in the London subway to protect it from bombs falling from German airplanes. In the early 1940s the Smithsonian Institution finally asked Orville Wright for the aircraft. Orville agreed, and in 1948 the *Flyer* came home.

In the Air and Space Museum the *Flyer* is the centerpiece of a breathtaking exhibit. The exhibit is called Milestones of Flight. It is an amazing collection of aircraft that have achieved historic "firsts" in aviation. In the middle of the exhibit is the *Flyer*, the first powered machine to fly. Hanging from the ceiling next to it is the *Spirit of St. Louis*. In 1927 it became the first aircraft to carry a solo pilot across the Atlantic Ocean. Also suspended nearby is the Bell *X-1*. In 1947 the *X-1* zoomed to the speed of 700 miles an hour to become the first aircraft to fly faster than sound. On the floor directly below the *Flyer* is the Apollo II spacecraft. Called the *Columbia*, this was the spacecraft flown in 1969 by the first men to walk on the moon.

At the Air and Space Museum, only twenty feet separate the *Flyer* from the *Columbia*. One craft carried Orville Wright on a 120-foot flight over a sandy field in North Carolina. The other craft carried three men to the moon and back. Sixty-six years divided the two events. Did the Wright brothers ever dream that development of their frail aircraft would someday lead to flight in space? No one knows. All a visitor to the museum can do is look with awe at the *Flyer* and then at the *Columbia* and wonder what aviation and mankind will achieve in the next sixty-six years.

It is often said that a journey of one thousand
miles begins with a single step. The Wright brothers
took that single step at Kitty Hawk in 1903.
Mankind is still on the journey.

About the Author

R. Conrad Stein was born and grew up in Chicago. He enlisted in the Marine Corps at the age of eighteen, and served for three years. He then attended the University of Illinois, where he received a Bachelor's Degree in history. He later studied in Mexico and earned a Master of Fine Arts degree from the University of Guanajuato.

The study of history is Mr. Stein's hobby. Since he finds it to be an exciting subject, he tries to bring the excitement of history to his readers. He is the author of many other books, articles, and short stories written for young people.

About the Artist

Len Meents studied painting and drawing at Southern Illinois University and after graduation in 1969 he moved to Chicago. Mr. Meents works full time as a painter and illustrator. He and his wife and child currently make their home in LaGrange, Illinois.